# *Wisdomisms*

# Wisdomisms

### A Daily Spirit-Guided Approach to Opening Up Your Life to Greater Possibilities

## Njambi G. Mungai

REGENT PRESS
Berkeley, California

Manufactured in the U.S.A.
REGENT PRESS
Berkeley, California
www.regentpress.net

**"-ism"** a suffix appearing in loanwords from Greek, where it was used to form action nouns from verbs (baptism); on this model, used as a productive suffix in the formation of nouns denoting action or practice, state or condition, principles, doctrines, a usage or characteristic, devotion or adherence, etc. (criticism; barbarism; Darwinism; despotism; plagiarism; realism; witticism; intellectualism). – Dictionary.com

**Wisdomism** came from a word I decided would sum up the type of inspirational thoughts that are shared in this book. If it were ever to become dictionary-worthy, it would be defined in two ways:

## Wisdomism

1. noun – a motivational statement or suggestion that promotes self-awareness and growth.
"I will read a wisdomism every day."
2. noun – the quality of being wise; an adherence to the practice of applying daily wisdom or inspiration to your life.
"I find myself practicing Wisdomism based on the guidance I've been getting from this book."

# *Dedications*

To my son, Brandon Mungai Phillips. When you left this earth, I somehow found a way to deepen my faith and stand up courageously and live despite the tremendous grief I felt. I was able to carry on because of the amazing gift you left us, your daughter, Leila Marisol.

To my beloved granddaughter, Leila Marisol Phillips. I grow in my ever-changing role as your grandmother as you grow into womanhood, one day at a time. You are my heart and soul and make my life so much more meaningful. You inspire me to be more and do more, and I am hoping that you will be as proud of me as I am of you.

To my "chosen" daughter, Tracy Mangles-Merrick, who was my son's beloved partner and is mother to my granddaughter. We were brought together in our now Mother/Daughter relationship through unbearable circumstances, but here we are! I could not be more grateful for you.

To my First family: my dear brother, John (Johnny) Woods; sister, Gwen (Cookie) Woods Spaulding; brother, Karl (Teddy) Woods; cousin, Salvador del Viento; and all my beloved cousins. Your love and support are the "glue" that kept our weirdly combined and loving family together. You are so precious to me. I love you way more than you know!

To my Kenyan family (siblings, uncle, aunts, and cousins). Your righteousness and grace shine through everything you do. How proud I am to be a part of you. I love you all!

To my Dutch family. Your acceptance of me in

your lives completed my circle and made me whole. I am grateful for the deep affection and love we share ... thank you!

To those dear souls, my angels, who were placed here with me so we could traverse our lives together through thick and thin: Thea Khama, Tonia Chapple, and Tanya Dennis (my three "T"s). May our journey never end!

To the grassroots organization called Soka Gakkai International (SGI-USA). Thank you for giving me a spiritual place to rest and enough intellectual stimulation to keep me interested and engaged with meaningful dialogue through following the tenets and practice of Nichiren Buddhism. My deepest gratitude goes to the third president of the SGI, Daisaku Ikeda, for being a peacemaker and a mentor to countless many. Through your example, you have shown me that I am capable of tapping into my limitless potential and that I *can* become happy.

To my on-earth spirit guide, Veronica LaBarrie. You helped me navigate *the worst* time of my life and gave me tools and strategies for living my best life through the practice of A Course in Miracles. I am eternally grateful for the unselfish gift of your time, mentorship, and counsel over those eight years and for our subsequent union as friends and family.

Finally, to my four beautiful, loving fur babies – who sometimes make life chaotic – but who remind me every day that *Life is Good!* And to my little five-pound powerhouse, Oliver Galileo, who left us just before this book was published, Mommy loves you.

# *Introduction*

I began writing *Wisdomisms* just after the turn of the 21st century. It took an outbreak of a virus unparalleled in insidious worldwide destruction, the likes of which have gone unseen for a hundred years, for me to decide that this was the right time to finish it. The precariousness and uncertainty of life during this frightening time jolted me out of my lethargy and spurred me back into action. So, what stopped me before the pandemic? It was the notion that I had plenty of time to write it and that I would eventually get around to it – one day.

When discussing my hesitation to finish this book, a dear friend gave me the sage wisdom that perhaps I was cautious because I was not ready to give this special part of me to you. Subconsciously, I think I wanted to hold onto this body of work which is very dear to me before releasing it to unknown eyes and hearts. Upon looking deeper, my reluctance to move forward with this book grew from my fear of what you might think about its content: Will you *get* what I am trying to say? Will you benefit from putting in the daily work? Although I do not know the answers, I now realize how important it is to allow *Wisdomisms* to find its way from a very special place in my heart into your hands and the hands of others who may be inspired by reading it. Therefore, finishing this labor of love became essential. And considering the Divine scheme of things, the *right time* happens to be *now*.

The intent of this book is to encourage positive thought. I want to inspire your heart and your soul to open up and expand your blessings and possibilities. Instead of honoring fear, I want you to choose to embrace what you will not allow yourself to be, do, or have; to grasp the dreams and aspirations you may not readily act on or rise to otherwise. I want you to access areas of your heart and soul that were previously inaccessible. My hope is that this book encourages you to reveal your Self in deeper, more vulnerable ways, all for the Greater Good. Give your Self permission to awaken your Spirit and mind and allow them to intersect into one magnificent ... and powerful ... and loving ... Being. This awakening comes with daily practice. Lastly, I hope that whatever drew you to this book will keep you curious about deepening your faith and discovering more about anything and everything that feeds your soul and makes you feel nourished and fulfilled.

Dear One, our journey is endless.

# *Faith*

Because I have faith, I am capable of comprehending life, eternal and mysterious.

Because I have faith, amid the ugly struggle for survival, I can stride, maintaining purity, through a victorious life.

Because I have faith, amid humanity bound by iron chains and imprisoned in the burning house, I can walk, in peace and tranquility, through a life of freedom.

Because I have faith, I can grasp life as the reality of eternity, happiness, true self and purity, and not illusory dreams born of transient phenomena.

Because I have faith, even in a society filled with contradictions and irrationality, I can advance boldly, confident in the law of cause and effect.

Because I have faith, I will not be moved even in the least by huge waves, for I have boarded the great ship of eternity.

Because I have faith, I can experience value, major good and vital life force, and the happiness of human revolution.

— DAISAKU IKEDA  p.75 A Youthful Diary

As far back as I can remember, I have always been a Spiritual person and a seeker of truth. In my adolescence I looked for answers to those beliefs that were commonly understood in the Christian world. I went to parochial schools for 12 years and by the time I was 17 and a junior in high school, I really began questioning the basic tenets and principles we Christians accepted wholeheartedly without ever asking how or why. For example: How was Jesus immaculately conceived? How was it possible for Him to feed thousands of people with a few loaves of bread and fish, walk on water, and rise from the dead? How does someone part a sea, get transformed into a pillar of salt, and accomplish so many other mind-boggling miraculous manifestations – all of which to me seemed impossible? As a 17-year-old still trying to make sense of the world, I was looking for more concrete facts, something I could wrap my head around. When I asked my religion teachers these questions – in earnest, mind you – they did not have answers I thought were logical or acceptable. The answers always fell back on what we were expected to accept without question – just agree to all of it on pure faith, without explanation.

Those were early lessons for me in faith. And at that time, when all else in my world had explanations, and formulas, and diagrams, and procedures, it became difficult for me to go along with these dogmas because they were 'just what we believe is true'. Hence, my journey for answers began. From there, I went on what I feel is now a decades-long journey to find a Spiritual place that felt comfortable, safe, nurturing, and one that I could understand. I explored places along this path that inspired mystical thought which gave way to different Spiritual perspectives. From what I now know, I have determined that some things must be accepted on pure faith. I recently found a quote from Mahatma Gandhi which says, "Faith is not something to grasp, it is a state to grow into."

Along with my desire to find my Spiritual comfort zone, I also learned that I had a deep desire to help others. I earned a Master of Science Degree in Clinical Psychology to fulfill this aspiration. For more than a decade I worked with children and adults through various consulting agreements I had with the Oakland Unified School District and the Peralta Community College District in California. I also trained for over a year to become a Certified Life Coach through a wonderful program called the Coach for Life Institute.

What makes the Coach for Life style of coaching unique is that I learned to work with clients in a way that had a direct impact on transforming the human spirit by addressing the most essential aspects of a person's heart and soul. This was accomplished by concentrating on three vital areas: a person's core values, their core life purpose, and their core strengths. This empowering practice embraced a holistic approach incorporating the mind, the body, and the spirit of our clients, paying particular attention to their positive traits with an effort to develop each of those areas. The creator of this program, Peter J. Reding, felt that when we are living our best life, we are actively living in perfect balance and alignment with our true, most authentic Self.

This experience was followed by the opportunity to spend eight years studying with an amazing Spiritual coach and celebrated author, Veronica Gabrielle La Barrie. I learned about a practice called A Course in Miracles (ACIM, or the Course). ACIM is primarily learned through self-study with the goal of finding the way to universal peace, happiness, and Love by releasing all guilt and finding forgiveness for Self and others. It teaches that fear and guilt can be overcome through miracles, which are defined as the highest manifestation of Love. The focus is on healing your Self by incorporating a daily practice of exercises from the workbook to change your perceptions and developing your own Internal Teacher for guidance. Although the language of the Course uses traditional Christian references, ACIM is a non-denominational, non-sectarian school of thought and is not considered a religion. The Spiritual truths by which I live today were cultivated while studying A Course in Miracles and built upon everything I have learned over the years.

I am currently a Nichiren Buddhist and have been practicing for two decades. Nichiren Buddhism is a branch of Mahayana Buddhism. It is our practice to chant *Nam Myoho Renge Kyo*

and follow the writings of Nichiren Daishonin,
a 13th century Japanese Buddhist priest who
developed these principles based on the Lotus
Sutra, which he considered the highest truth of
Buddhist teachings. His basic belief was that these
teachings are accessible to all men and women
equally, which was a great departure from the
teachings and beliefs of other Buddhist sects at
that time. It is a practice from which *all* people can
benefit – not just the selected few. We believe that
all people can become happy. This higher level
of consciousness can be accomplished through
chanting *Nam Myoho Renge Kyo*. Chanting this
mantra is a form of oral meditation that opens up a
connection to the Universe. It allows practitioners
to transform themselves to become happy in
all aspects of their lives and enables them to
connect with their limitless potential, wisdom, and
compassion and create value for themselves and
others.

I find that I am now satisfied with this Spiritual place and I have found a home within one of the Nichiren Buddhist lay movements called Soka Gakkai International (SGI) - USA. However, I also view myself as someone with a broader perspective on Spirituality where there is no one *true* way. What really matters is if we come from a place of Love and live a life that upholds the Universal Truths about what is right and good, the world ultimately becomes better.

I am much older and wiser now, and having evolved from my rebellious teen years, I now believe that unwavering faith and acceptance of an indisputable connection to a Power beyond our comprehension is the common thread that connects every living thing in this Universe. It is a Power which emanates from our Spiritual Center, our Heart, our Soul – in fact, from the very essence of our Being. This Power is who we truly are, our Authentic Self; an essence inside that sets us apart from other living beings and enables us not only to choose right from wrong but to expand our limited world view to greater divine-centered heights. Whatever the Divine Essence is called – Source, Spirit, God, Buddha, Yahweh, Jehovah, the Universe, the Soul, Magnificence, Love ... among other names, *It* cannot be denied. We are one with *It*. *It is us! It* makes us who we are. We can tap into *Its* power and brilliance at any given point. To live our best life and be the very best human being we can, we must strive to create a permanent and indestructible bond with this Internal and Eternal Resource. Throughout this book, I will refer to *It* in many ways because for me, there is no one name to describe this Almighty Ever-Presence that we all know and cannot deny.

When I started writing these words of inspiration, my daily habit was to jot down at least five things I was grateful for every day, using what Oprah Winfrey called a "Gratitude Journal."

Moreover, I would start with a simple statement of divinely inspired self-guidance that I was motivated to write in that moment. I sat quietly allowing my mind to be still and let the thoughts come through me without trying to create or force the words, and they would just flow. These inspirations and ones that have emerged since my journaling days are what I'd like to share with you now.

The closer I come to *my* Internal and Eternal Wisdom, the more I recognize and acknowledge what my true mission is in life. My mission is to encourage and inspire others to be their best Self, to live life without fear, and to open their hearts and minds to the Greater Good.

My greatest desire is that you use *Wisdomisms* to propel your life toward infinite possibilities and everlasting happiness.

Wishing you many Blessings, Love, and Light

*Wisdomisms*

NOTES: You may notice that some of these inspirations may recur paraphrased or repeated. My intention is that you revisit certain ideas that are worth repeating to focus more attention on these concepts.

For words that you find unfamiliar, please refer to the Glossary of Terms on page 326.

HELPFUL TIP: Focus on just one wisdomism each day. After reading it, sit with your wisdomism for a few minutes, and give your Self the space and time to let this guidance sink in. Then, consciously choose to hold onto this thought throughout your day.

By following this procedure every day, my prayer is that over time you will become more in touch with your true Self and more spiritually energized and aware. Most importantly, you will rid yourself of the dead wood that has been holding you back from becoming the best person you can be!

*Today I will …*

*open my heart and interact with people in a loving way*

*Today I will …*

*make sure my thoughts
are directed and clear,
and my heart listen
intently for the right
guidance from my
Spiritual Center*

*Today I will …*

*connect with my Center
on a heart level and
know what it is I need
so I can move forward*

*Today I will …*

*be still and listen
to guidance from
my Essence*

*Today I will …*

*be in the present and focused on NOW*

*Today I will …*

*work on clarity, on having good intentions, and focus on attaining inner peace*

*Today I will ...*

*enjoy a clear,
Spirit-guided day*

*Today I will …*

*walk as one with
my higher Self*

*Today I will ...*

*know my Self
and stay in Spirit*

*Today I will ...*

*find that place of
balance within*

*Today I will ...*

*remain focused in my Light and true goodness*

*Today I will ...*

*commit to walk in Spirit, keeping all ego-driven thoughts out of reach*

*Today I will ...*

*become stronger in my Spirituality as this is my right path*

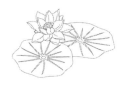

*Today I will …*

*be at peace and choose to have no outwardly negative emotions*

*Today I will ...*

*enter this day with
a softness and kind-
Spiritedness toward my
Self and others*

*Today I will …*

*find joy and
Light-Hearted-ness
in all that I do*

*Today I will …*

*meet the challenge to calm my Self, be still, and open my Self to receive wisdom, guidance, and Love*

*Today I will …*

*stay in Spirit, removing all anger, and approach this day with Love*

*Today I will …*

*remain in a state that is open for guidance*

*Today I will ...*

*be aware of connections; to my Self, to others, to Spirit*

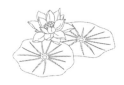

*Today I will ...*

*choose to be loving
and kind to everyone
I encounter*

*Today I will …*

*BE in this day without outer interference or internal upset*

*Today I will …*

*experience joy
in my heart*

*Today I will …*

*allow peace to be part of each moment*

*Today I will …*

## *BE in a state of peace and in harmony with the Greater Good*

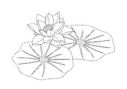

*Today I will …*

*go forth with a loving, accepting attitude*

*Today I will …*

*welcome this day
filled with joy and
a wonderful sense
of possibility*

*Today I will …*

*realize there is an eternal connection between my Self, all humanity, and all living things*

*Today I will …*

*remind my Self all day of my Spiritual Source and my connection to it*

*Today I will …*

*tap into my Spiritual Source and know that I BE all that I AM*

*Today I will ...*

*practice the perfect, peaceful state of BE-ing*

*Today I will …*

*be brave and open
to learn and grow
with every breath
and prosper from every
In-Between moment*

*Today I will …*

*journey safely and enjoy
the small pleasures*

*Today I will …*

*be grounded, but uplifted and appreciate those around me*

*Today I will …*

*go forth with clarity and
assurance that I AM*

*Today I will …*

*greet this day with enthusiasm for all the wonderful blessings there are to enjoy*

*Today I will ...*

*appreciate everything that is here for me*

*Today I will …*

*realize there are blessings that come to me that are not so obvious. I am grateful for my Inconspicuous Blessings, too*

*Today I will …*

*recognize the many
forms in which Spirit is
providing guidance and
offering blessings*

*Today I will …*

*release all of my ideas
of convention and
accept all that comes
to me is right for me*

*Today I will ...*

*go forth with a
positive attitude, a
richness of Spirit, and a
true connection to
my Magnificence*

*Today I will …*

*look for peace and ease
in everything I do*

*Today I will ...*

*focus on peace in my heart and see only that which brings peace in my life*

*Today I will …*

*take a moment to bring my thoughts back in line with the truth of who I AM*

*Today I will ...*

*walk in the Light with all my efforts focused on peace*

*Today I will …*

*find gratitude
in my attitude*

*Today I will …*

*constantly be aware
of my connection to
Spirit and to the joy and
happiness associated
with that*

*Today I will …*

*bond in faith and trust with my Source*

*Today I will ...*

*be grateful for the opportunity to bring positive change into my life*

*Today I will …*

*know that I am in my right and perfect place and I am okay*

*Today I will ...*

*know that all my needs
will be abundantly met
without fail*

Today I will …

*fill my life and my heart with possibility, Love, and Light*

*Today I will …*

*be loving, giving, and sharing; show my true Self to all*

*Today I will ...*

*connect with Source
right now and just BE*

*Today I will …*

*only draw things to me
that serve and honor me*

*Today I will …*

*remain focused and in the Light*

*Today I will …*

*find harmony
in all that I do*

*Today I will …*

*see the joy and magic
in each moment.
Do not miss it!*

*Today I will ...*

*allow the Universe to provide me with all I need and all I want*

*Today I will …*

*go forth with the
conviction and
strength of a lion*

*Today I will …*

*know **I** am protected from all harm*

*Today I will ...*

*always BE in a loving state*

*Today I will …*

*walk in the truth of who I AM*

*Today I will ...*

*only see the
overwhelming beauty
in everything*

*Today I will …*

*only see the beauty of
the people I encounter*

*Today I will …*

*pay particular attention to who I BE while focusing on connecting to Spirit at all times*

*Today I will ...*

*allow the Guidance
to be heard —
listen carefully*

*Today I will …*

*let kindness prevail;
lead with an open,
loving heart*

*Today I will ...*

*know that all positive change in my life starts with me*

*Today I will …*

*keep my eye on the Light. Move daily in that direction*

*Today I will ...*

*be fair and honest
with everyone*

*Today I will …*

*work on eliminating judgement completely*

*Today I will ...*

*listen to Guidance,*
*stay focused*

*Today I will …*

*know that there are
no fears except those
I create*

*Today I will ...*

*handle any fear and trepidation because my I AM is bigger than my fears*

*Today I will …*

*be sustained by Love*

*Today I will …*

*become a seeker of Universal Light and Internal Guidance*

*Today I will …*

*move forward with peace and happiness*

*Today I will ...*

*choose to be in gratitude for the many gifts I receive each day*

*Today I will …*

*connect with Source
knowing that I AM*

*Today I will …*

*focus on clarity
and what IS.
Make the connection*

*Today I will …*

*be grateful for
family and friends
who love me*

*Today I will ...*

*make a commitment
to support my own
progress in this journey*

*Today I will …*

*surrender with Love
and gratitude because I
know that Spirit is
my Source*

*Today I will …*

*decide that correct thinking is powerful and addicting*

*Today I will …*

*dig deep for my Truth
because the Truth will
set me free*

*Today I will …*

*choose to be the one who makes a difference*

*Today I will …*

*in gratitude, stand and await guidance from my Source. I am an open channel to receive*

*Today I will …*

*enjoy and savor each moment of this day knowing that it is all a gift to me*

*Today I will …*

*choose **Light**
over darkness*

*Today I will …*

*go forth with an open
heart and a loving Spirit*

*Today I will …*

*give freely and know that the only thing that is real is Love*

Today I will ...

*become a Light Bearer. I hold the torch that lights the path for those seeking their way*

*Today I will …*

*choose to see, to know, to feel, to BE in connection with Spirit. Today, nothing else matters*

*Today I will …*

*walk in remembrance
of these divine words …
Truth and Love are
all there is*

*Today I will ...*

*embrace this day as mine. What I choose to do with it is either divinely inspired or not*

*Today I will ...*

*choose to flourish
and prosper*

*Today I will …*

*listen to my inner guidance*

*Today I will ...*

*be open, be receptive.
Only I can recognize the
Light within. Know it
is there ... always*

*Today I will …*

*choose to be victorious in everything I do*

*Today I will ...*

*be an open channel
to receive the gifts
and inspirations that
are mine*

*Today I will ...*

*integrate what I know
is true into my DOing
so that I can BE at
peace and in harmony*

*Today I will ...*

*release old thoughts, habits and patterns. Clean the slate and be still*

*Today I will …*

*know the Truth will come and fill the empty space. It was always there*

*Today I will …*

*focus and commit to remaining open, which are two important components on the journey toward enLightenment*

*Today I will …*

*find the Light and bask in it. Let it warm my entire body and soul*

*Today I will ...*

*focus on Spiritual and physical healing and regeneration*

*Today I will …*

*celebrate in knowing there is absolutely NOTHING I cannot do!*

*Today I will …*

*be a sterling example
of goodness, kindness
and love for others*

*Today I will ...*

*listen for guidance
and ask for forgiveness
if necessary*

*Today I will ...*

*forgive myself*

*Today I will …*

*decide that all my actions begin with Love before I act*

*Today I will …*

*be at peace, be loving, thoughtful and kind — be free to experience a beautiful life*

*Today I will ...*

*regard each day as a blessing, an opportunity, and an adventure*

*Today I will ...*

*commit to treat others
with respect and Love*

*Today I will ...*

*be still before speaking
or acting. Make sure
that my I AM
is present*

*Today I will ...*

*honor Clarity,
Peacefulness,
and Love*

*Today I will …*

*determine that each moment must be lived as though it is a final performance — because it is*

*Today I will …*

*strengthen my
connection to my family*

*Today I will …*

*allow others to see my Light and let it shine brightly enough so that they recognize theirs*

*Today I will ...*

*know that everything I do comes from Love*

*Today I will …*

*attract all that I deserve in my life*

*Today I will …*

*be the best person I can be every day. Never cheat my Self or others out of this gift*

*Today I will …*

*listen to my inner Guidance. Learn to be quiet, open my heart, and just receive*

*Today I will …*

*see all things work out regarding my life as it is Divinely designed*

*Today I will …*

*maintain my strength in my connection to Spirit and my commitment to Self while pursuing the Light*

*Today I will …*

*hear my guidance at all times. Concentrate on LISTENING*

*Today I will …*

*know that through
my honesty and
forthrightness
THE WAY will
be shown*

*Today I will ...*

*find incredible joy in everything I do*

*Today I will …*

*love my Self first
before all else*

*Today I will ...*

*live completely as my true Self knowing that when I do, honesty and righteousness prevail*

*Today I will …*

*know that fear has no place in my heart. Love is all there is*

*Today I will …*

*prepare my Self
for all the goodness
the Universe has in
store for me*

*Today I will ...*

*go within, acknowledge Spirit, and act on any guidance that might reveal itself*

*Today I will …*

*become more rooted in my Spiritual connection and assist those around me to do the same*

*Today I will …*

*experience comfort and joy in the magnificent beauty and the everlasting Light in my life*

*Today I will ...*

*enjoy each moment every day, regarding it as though it is a gift, because it is!*

*Today I will ...*

*know my Self*
*Love my Self*
*Honor my Self*

*Today I will ...*

*focus on healing my Self — both inside and out*

*Today I will …*

*be all for others that
I would be for
my Self*

*Today I will …*

*be all for my Self that
I would be for others*

*Today I will …*

*feel a sweet soothing
balm enveloping my
body and soul —
bringing comfort
and peace*

*Today I will …*

*focus only on the Light in my life*

*Today I will …*

*be aware that shadows in darkness will always attempt to overpower, but now I am not available to it*

*Today I will ...*

*be fierce, courageous and ready to take on those things I perceive as challenges*

*Today I will …*

## know that *I* can make things happen, perfectly, as they should be

*Today I will ...*

*be in full connection
with Spirit. There are
no concerns or problems
when I live there*

*Today I will …*

*always find that place
of peace and inspiration
in each moment*

*Today I will ...*

*behold the miracles in store for me. What a wonderful thing!*

*Today I will …*

*focus on wholeness,
of Self, of life, of
relationships, of Love*

*Today I will ...*

*listen to my Self, what my body and Spirit are telling me, and follow the guidance*

*Today I will …*

*be open.*
*Be in the moment.*
*Be free to receive*
*the goodness I deserve.*
*Be willing to share*
*with others*

*Today I will …*

*feel peaceful.*
*Encourage others.*
*Live in the Light*

*Today I will …*

*embrace each day
as new — just as
each moment is new.
Celebrate the gifts that
each moment in each
day brings*

*Today I will …*

*remember that happiness and joy are necessary ingredients in the recipe of Life*

*Today I will …*

*break through these self-imposed bonds of inadequacy and self-contempt and embrace my I AM*

*Today I will* …

*choose to celebrate my life as it is right now*

*Today I will …*

*choose one person to encourage and inspire*

*Today I will …*

*appreciate the newness
of each moment*

*Today I will …*

*look at gratitude as
an attitude that must
be embraced in each
moment every day*

*Today I will …*

*see that Love and
happiness are the
key elements to life;
anything outside of
that is not real*

*Today I will …*

*know that Peace is the essence of the Soul's happiness. Find and maintain all ways to support that state of being*

*Today I will …*

*give what **I** have of my Self to others*

*Today I will …*

*find that as I discover the Light, I must let it shine through*

*Today I will ...*

*embrace complete
forgiveness and Love
for others, it brings me
closer to the Light*

*Today I will ...*

*be everything I was created to be.*
*Life is short*

*Today I will ...*

*recognize that Life is simple. It is our thoughts about it that make it complicated*

*Today I will …*

*realize that my feelings
and emotions are not
to be stifled as they are
truly an expression of
life and how **I** live it*

*Today I will ...*

*appreciate that inner guidance is the beacon of Light that shows us the way. Listening to it keeps us on our path and prevents us from running ashore*

*Today I will …*

*maintain a sense of peace and harmony. It is easy to do when there is a strong connection to Spirit*

*Today I will …*

*strive to fulfill my commitments and enjoy the peace and serenity around this accomplishment*

*Today I will …*

*find peace and tranquility in each moment every day. The less I search for it the easier it is to find*

*Today I will ...*

*get my head out of the way and let my heart lead the way*

*Today I will …*

*recognize that my soul is not a part of my body — it is eternal — just as Spirit is. They are aligned as one*

*Today I will …*

*understand that I am free to be my magnificent Self*

*Today I will ...*

*wait for Guidance before making any decisions*

*Today I will …*

*live in a place of knowing that I am worthy of receiving all the goodness I deserve*

*Today I will ...*

*be guided by the heart
... always take a
moment to listen*

*Today I will …*

*go forth without fear
or hesitation because
I know I am protected
and Spirit is always
with me*

*Today I will ...*

*enjoy the marvelous
feeling of wellness
in mind and body —
work toward maintaining
and growing that sense
of BEing*

*Today I will ...*

*focus on purity
of thought*

*Today I will …*

*seize the wonderful and blessed moments that come to me as gifts*

*Today I will ...*

*bring peace not only to my Self, but also to my environment and to the world*

*Today I will ...*

*regard my fears as opportunities to grow, to love unconditionally, and to live freely*

*Today I will ...*

*embrace the idea that happiness, contentment, peacefulness, Light, smiles, and connection are all aligned with Spirit*

Today I will …

*decide not to give up
my power to things
like worry and concern
— when they show up
is when strength and
conviction must prevail*

*Today I will ...*

*understand that fear kills all connections with my Oneness. It pulls me away from the Light and back into darkness*

*Today I will ...*

*recognize that life is precious and we must respect and appreciate it*

*Today I will ...*

*focus on what is most important, which is the Light, Spirit, and the I AM*

*Today I will …*

*experience the pleasure
that Nature provides.
It is such a glorious
background on the
canvas of life*

*Today I will ...*

*listen to my heart, my inner guidance, my Life. There is no flaw in what I hear*

*Today I will ...*

*forgive. It is the key
to salvation*

*Today I will …*

*hold space for this new day with my focus on what is happening in each moment. Celebrate the newness! Celebrate what IS*

*Today I will …*

*explore the creativity within for it is manifested divinity*

Today I will …

*declare that I am healthy. When the mind is healthy, so is the body. Today, these two are in complete harmony*

*Today I will …*

*listen carefully and never second guess what I hear. Inspiration comes from deep within*

*Today I will ...*

*celebrate family —
the specialness and
uniqueness of mine.
The ones who come
together as family do
not do so by accident.
Why was I blessed
with those around me?*

*Today I will …*

*focus on my own
magnificent greatness.
I am one with Spirit
and all that I do is a
reflection of that*

*Today I will ...*

*let Divine Guidance flow through me releasing the brilliance of wisdom*

*Today I will ...*

*find the time to be quiet
and listen to my heart*

*Today I will …*

*concentrate on the beauty in everything I see*

*Today I will ...*

*find the courage to
offer others my
sacred inner Light*

*Today I will …*

*extend Love to everyone I encounter*

*Today I will ...*

*acknowledge that judgement blocks Light and Love*

*Today I will …*

*receive any and all communication from Source with an open heart*

*Today I will …*

*recognize and maintain the connection between mind, body, and Spirit. This combination represents wholeness, and wholeness leads to enLightenment*

*Today I will …*

*go forth knowing that every person **I** encounter or think about is first met with Love*

*Today I will …*

*embrace any challenge I have and turn it into an opportunity to face it with the courage of a lion and to become victorious over it*

*Today I will …*

*let the Love in my heart
shine through in each
and every encounter
with others*

*Today I will …*

*know that Love is the medicine for all that ails. Love is present in each moment; I just have to recognize it*

*Today I will …*

*connect to Source and follow the guidance that comes from this powerful alliance*

*Today I will …*

*see the beauty in
everything my eyes meet*

*Today I will …*

*not let fear interfere
with my happiness*

*Today I will …*

*be vigilant and allow my mind to serve my highest good. My thoughts become my reality*

*Today I will ...*

*keep on smiling – even when I do not think there is a reason to, there is*

*Today I will …*

*be kind and gentle
with my Self*

*Today I will ...*

*look to the Universe for harmony. Look to Nature for harmony. Look WITHIN for harmony*

*Today I will …*

*embrace the peace
and knowingness that
wherever I am, I AM*

*Today I will …*

*see that there is a gift
in each moment.
Is that not a marvelous
thing to know?*

*Today I will ...*

*dance to the soulful music of harmony, peace, inspiration, and Love*

*Today I will …*

*appreciate that being charitable means giving when I do not believe I have it in me to give*

Today I will …

*BE in the world
knowing that I have the
opportunity to create
each moment*

*Today I will ...*

*be mindful that
connection to Source
is the most important
connection there is*

*Today I will …*

*be open to all
possibilities*

*Today I will ...*

*know that everything is not always as it seems. Our perceptions are colored by our beliefs*

*Today I will …*

*be a sponge. However, I will take in only that which serves me*

*Today I will ...*

*listen to and follow
through on my
inspirations*

*Today I will ...*

*find that place of
peace and stillness
within and celebrate
the magnificence of
the moment*

*Today I will ...*

*let my guard down —*
*take a risk —*
*open my heart*

*Today I will …*

*celebrate each moment. Focus on what IS right now, not what was or will be*

*Today I will …*

*find a higher place
to dwell when I am
weighed down with
matters of the heart*

*Today I will …*

*first, Love my Self.
Then recognize that
everyone around me
IS me*

*Today I will …*

*appreciate the gift in everything my eyes rest upon*

*Today I will …*

*always keep my faith strong. It nourishes the Spirit and the Soul*

*Today I will ...*

*lead the day with my kind and loving heart*

*Today I will …*

*be the pebble that creates ripples of goodness in this world. It all starts with me!*

*Today I will …*

*give like there is no tomorrow. Generosity comes from the heart*

*Today I will …*

*remember my divine connection with Spirit*

*Today I will …*

*be at peace, in harmony, and in a loving space*

*Today I will …*

*show others my Light from within through my patience, kindness, and warmth*

*Today I will ...*

*open my life to perfect
happiness by forgiving
my Self and others*

*Today I will …*

*enjoy this day with Love, family, and much happiness*

*Today I will ...*

*embrace NOW. It is all we have — do not waste precious moments*

*Today I will …*

*BE in a state of peace and happiness*

*Today I will ...*

*regard ALL Creation with the utmost Love and respect*

Today I will …

*focus on the 98% that
is working in my life —
not the 2% that is not*

*Today I will ...*

*check the sincerity
and the source of my
feelings. Make sure they
are genuine and not
manufactured by the ego*

*Today I will …*

*follow my heart.*
*Discover my passion.*
*Live … completely*

*Today I will ...*

*recognize that Life is easy. We make it difficult through our erroneous thinking*

*Today I will …*

*be patient. The gift of age is wisdom*

*Today I will ...*

*give in to the joy I have in life — do not dwell on what is joyless*

*Today I will ...*

*learn that when I change my Self, I change the environment around me*

*Today I will ...*

*allow Divine Inspiration to flow through me in all that I do*

*Today I will …*

*manifest only that which I truly want, need, and desire for my Life*

*Today I will ...*

*align with Spirit, it makes me unstoppable*

*Today I will …*

*transform my perceived challenges into opportunities; to realign my thinking which gives way to growth and prosperity*

*Today I will* ...

*be present in this moment. I will not allow the past or future to spoil the magnificence of NOW*

*Today I will …*

*experience LOVE from everywhere with a fresh attitude, like I am feeling it for the first time … even if it is not*

*Today I will ...*

*extend my Love and connection to others without reserve or hesitation*

*Today I will …*

*seek only what is true
and right for me*

*Today I will ...*

*make an effort to let
my family and friends
know I love them.
I will strengthen the
bonds that connect us*

*Today I will …*

*stop before I take action and ask my Self how I would respond if I were aligned with Spirit*

*Today I will ...*

*see that peace and joy
can be found in each
and every moment*

*Today I will …*

*make my eyes the windows to my soul. My encounters with everyone will be Spirit-filled and meaningful so that they can see who I truly AM*

*Today I will …*

*let my Light shine
as bright as possible*

*Today I will …*

*bask in the fullness, the richness, the warmth of Divine Love inside me*

*Today I will ...*

*feel whole*

*Today I will …*

*become a Spirit-guided
Beacon of hope, Love,
joy, happiness, and
kindness this day
and every day*

*Today I will ...*

*celebrate the
magnificence and
wonder of all the gifts
on earth I have to enjoy*

*Today I will …*

*let my connection to
Spirit warm my heart
and soul like the sun
warms my face
and body*

*Today I will …*

*love, nurture, and pamper my Self all day*

*Today I will …*

*let my Self feel EVERYthing, then acknowledge all my feelings with Love and move on*

*Today I will …*

*accept the Love that comes to me with open arms*

*Today I will …*

*focus on being in the moment … allow for no past or future distractions*

*Today I will ...*

*be free to trust my walk
with Spirit*

*Today I will …*

*still the noise —*
*hear the symphony*

*Today I will …*

*allow the Light to be reborn in me every day*

*Today I will …*

*find opportunities to be with my Self.*
*Quiet time brings blessed moments*

*Today I will* …

*recognize that being judgmental is harsh and unnecessary. This is not who I AM*

*Today I will …*

*always follow
those sudden urges
to reach out to others —
it is just Spirit giving me
a little nudge*

*Today I will …*

*avoid closing the door to my heart. Closing it is easy — it is reopening it that is so very difficult*

*Today I will …*

*see that endings are beginnings*

*Today I will ...*

*remember that fear is poison*

*Today I will …*

*maintain my connection
to Spirit by the way
I interact with each
person I encounter*

*Today I will ...*

*embrace the idea that good intentions are just that — good intentions. I must actualize them!*

*Today I will …*

*control my thoughts.
Do not let my thoughts
control me*

*Today I will ...*

*share some of my Light
with others*

*Today I will …*

*focus on knowing
that my Life is not as
complicated as I believe
it is. I will not muddle
the Truth with doubtful
thinking*

*Today I will ...*

*stop the blaring din of noise in my head — be still. Heaven awaits!*

*Today I will …*

*open my Self to accept that fear has no place in my life; only I have the power to change fear to courage*

*Today I will …*

*prepare to be surprised at the change I will experience in my outer world once I change my inner world*

*Today I will …*

*gratefully embrace knowing that Love is all there is*

*Today I will …*

*let a complete sense of peace exist in my heart*

*Today I will ...*

*know that without Love, there is no faith. Without faith, there is no life*

*Today I will …*

*accept that this is MY Life. I am here to Act it! Live it! BE it!*

# Inspirational Quotes from
# A Course in Miracles

When I have forgiven myself and
remembered who I am,
I will bless everyone
and everything I see.

W-PI.52.2:5 *A Course in Miracles*
THOUGHTS FROM THE FOUNDATION FOR INNER PEACE

. . . beauty will rise to bless your sight as you look upon
the world with forgiving eyes.

fT-17.11.6:1 *A Course in Miracles*
Thoughts from the Foundation for Inner Peace

# Glossary of Terms

**BE/I BE:** To BE is a state of mind. It is a safe space where you have a sense of peace and tranquility both inside and out, without the interruption of your ongoing inner chatter and chaos.

**Convention:** The usual society-driven thought. The way in which things are customarily done, in this case, in life. It is nothing more than just the cut-and-dried status quo.

**I AM:** The magnificent inner place of power that is fused with the Universe; the recognition of your Eternal Being as part of the Greater Good.

**In-Between moment:** Those times when you are not consciously focused on anything. This is a sacred space that is akin to transcendental consciousness. For a full definition of Transcendental Consciousness, go to: https://encyclopedia.uia.org/en/development/12320200

**Self (your Self; my Self):** Your Sacred Self. That part of you that is connected to Spirit. Your most vulnerable and pure Self.

**Spirit:** You *are* Spirit. That part of you that is Divine and Eternal; your connection to the Universe and all its Magnificence, Magic, Miracles, and Love. It is that lofty, untouchable place where you are the I AM. Christians believe in their oneness with God in recognition of the God-self. God is in all of us.

# *Additional Readings*

Daishonin, Nichiren. *The Writings of Nichiren Daishonin.* Soka Gakkai, 1999.

The Winning Life: *An Introduction to Buddhist Practice.* World Tribune Press, 2016.

Causton, Richard. *The Buddha in Daily Life: An introduction to the Buddhism of Nichiren Daishonin.* Random House, 1995.

Matsudo, Yukio. *Transform Your Energy – Change Your Life!:* Nichiren Buddhism 3.0. DPI Publishing, 2016.

Schucman, Dr. Helen. *A Course in Miracles.* Foundations for Inner Peace, 2007.

La Barrie, Veronica Gabrielle. *Things to Know about A Course in Miracles.* La Barrie Retreats, 2012.

La Barrie, Veronica Gabrielle. *Ungluing the Mind.* Balboa Press, 2018.

Williamson, Marianne. *A Return to Love: Reflections on the Principles of "A Course in Miracles".* HarperOne, 1996.

Reding, Peter J. *Positively Brilliant Self-mastery: Reclaim Your Authentic Self Now.* Positively Brilliant Productions, 2008.

# *About The Author*

Njambi G. Mungai has been President and Chief Executive Officer of JR Lester & Associates, Ltd. since 1992. As an entrepreneur based in Oakland, California, Ms. Mungai is a joint venture partner with several airport retail concessions companies in the Bay Area. For nearly twenty years, she owned and operated several popular retail and foodservice franchises in Oakland and San Francisco. She has a Master's of Science degree in Clinical Psychology, a work history in business and education, is a certified personal and professional life coach, and she completed an entrepreneurial training program at UC Berkeley's Haas School of Business. In addition, Njambi is and has been a member of several community groups and organizations associated with education, environment, health, the arts, and literacy. Most importantly, Njambi has the privilege of being called Grandmother by a very special young lady who is the light of her life. She also claims the title of "Dog Mom" to four adorable little pups.

# COMING SOON!

## *If You Only Live Long Enough ...*
## *a collection of light bulb moments*
presents basic common sense notions that are not
always commonly known and sometimes take
decades to figure out.
This book captures life's light bulb moments
for you rather than you having to
spend years waiting to arrive at
the same conclusions yourself.